The
LAKE DISTRICT

First published in Great Britain in 1998 by
Colin Baxter Photography Ltd.
Grantown-on-Spey,
Moray PH26 3NA

BT PG BH BH VCR SP BH CADCCVV SP BP FL BD

A CIP catalogue record for this book is available from the British Library

ISBN I 900455 29 3

Printed in Hong Kong

Front Cover Photograph: Great Gable, Sca Fell and Scafell Pike across Wast Water.
Back Cover Photograph: Stickle Ghyll and Lingmoor Fell.
Page One Photograph: Watendlath Tarn.
Page Three Photograph: Herdwick Sheep.

The
LAKE DISTRICT

Colin Baxter

Colin Baxter Photography, Grantown-on-Spey, Scotland

YEWBARROW, GREAT GABLE AND LINGMELL ACROSS WAST WATER

The Lake District

One April evening, at the end of a terrific walk up and over a mountain called Yewbarrow, we stood on the shore of Wast Water in the southwest corner of England's most beautiful National Park, The Lake District. In the silence golden waves of light flowed in slow motion over the sentinel mountains of Great Gable, Sca Fell, and Scafell Pike, their reflections gently shimmering on the surface of the lake.

The sense of space and calm almost spelled perfection and yet this is a part of one of the most densely populated countries in the northern hemisphere. The no through road alongside Wast Water is, however, a little more out of the way than most of the Lake District's thoroughfares. It retains a serenity that is sometimes lacking in other corners of this National Park, which is generally under enormous pressure from people. Understandably everyone, it seems, wishes to sample that feeling of just being within this very special landscape — a rich blend of fells, dales, villages and freshwater lakes. It was the combined quality of all these things that led to the designation of 880 square miles as a National Park in 1951. William Wordsworth, who made his home here, is widely credited with being a major influence in the original conception of National Parks in Great Britain. He said of the Lake District that it was a '…sort of national property in which every man has a right and interest who has an eye to perceive and a heart to enjoy'. Since the age of the Railway, tourists have been flocking to 'the Lakes' and considerable development has taken place within the last 150 years. Today the Lake District National Park attracts over eleven million staying visitor days per year.

Man has lived amongst the Cumbrian mountains for over 5000 years and there have been significant finds of prehistoric remains in the area. There is still visible evidence of Roman occupation in the early centuries AD, notably Hardknott Fort and High Street Roman road. The Anglo Saxons cleared much of the native forest that once clad the lower slopes of the central fells where they established settlements, and many Norse place names remain, evidence of early colonisation from Scandinavia.

During the Medieval period a more structured development took place. Stone walls appeared and further clearance of woodland for agriculture led in turn to the development of villages and towns. Mining and quarrying became important economically, and as far back as the eighteenth century roofing slate was extracted from the fells. The Lake District we see now started to take shape. Indeed the landscape is, in appearance, as much man-made as it is natural. It is the blend of all that character that has been created for functional purposes, mixed in with the grandeur of mountains sweeping down to lakes, each one with its own identity, that is so compelling. There is however one final ingredient, one usually in great abundance, which transforms all these features into an ever-changing theatre of light and land, and that is the weather.

On a clear blue sky day in the summer the landscape can have a perfection that is attractive in its own right. I have often felt though, that on such days the Lake District fells appear as cardboard cut-outs, until the sun lowers towards the western horizon and gradually their third dimension reappears and those very same fells are given some shape. But in the winter, although the colour green has disappeared from all but the very lower slopes and dale bottoms, the low angular rays of light sculpt the land with a warmth belying the temperature, often magnifying the unique character of the land.

When snow falls the Lake District dons a beauty that rivals any still summer day, but I think it is in the autumn that the fells, dales, lakes and tarns are at their best. A myriad of colour takes over; bracken, grasses and broadleaved woodland all shout their individual presence with an array of browns, yellows, oranges and reds. Green remains too, and blue in both the sky and water of course, and somewhere you will find every imaginable shade of grey, mauve and beige. When it rains all these colours are indescribably enriched and I have often stood dripping in my waterproofs feeling glad to witness the transformation of the landscape by water. After all there would not be the becks, tarns and lakes without the rain.

These photographs represent my view of what it feels like to be in this National Park through the changing seasons. There are many places, both high and low, which are not represented; I have simply chosen my favourite pictures from where I have been, and indeed I am one of the many million visitors for whom the Lake District has a special magic and attraction.

I often wonder though about the long-term effect of my boots on the slopes of the mountains and on the delicate meadows of the dales. One such meadow I know well in Little Langdale has a path right down the middle of it. Ten years ago the path was green yet visible, with a sign by the gate to the road identifying this field as a Site of Special Scientific Interest, and a brief statement referring to protected wild flower species found in meadows. Now just a decade later of ever-increasing popularity, the path is broad and brown and on a weekend throughout much of the summer season there is hardly ten minutes at a time when there is not a group of walkers crossing that meadow.

The pressure on the land is enormous. The thousands of climbers who conquer England's highest peak, Scafell Pike, each year have collectively eroded a wide gully such that it now appears as a rushing river of rock, and the scar of the path to Skiddaw's summit towering above Keswick can be seen from over twenty miles away. It is not only the fells that are under pressure though. Ninety percent of all visitors travel to and around the Lake District by car and many roads, big and small, are often so badly jammed with traffic that the very character of the place is, to some extent, spoiled.

This is a very fragile environment and the need for conservation of the many natural habitats and wealth of historic man-made features in the landscape has never been stronger. Thankfully there appears to be a greater awareness of these problems now, coupled with a general will to conserve the beauty and integrity of not just the Lake District but of all the National Parks of England and elsewhere. How we actually achieve this whilst still using them to such a degree raises a whole realm of issues and questions. Many people, however, expect to be free to go anywhere and for it to be free of charge. Perhaps, as in other parts of the world, even a nominal charge to visit the National Park would help towards the resources required to maintain it.

The endurance of such a beautiful place for generations to come is so very important, and I certainly hope that one way or another, many more people will watch the inevitable replays of that golden light on the fells across Wast Water.

Colin Baxter

LITTLE LANGDALE FROM PIKE OF BLISCO

WRAY CASTLE AND WINDERMERE

RYDAL WATER

BLENCATHRA

10

DERWENT WATER AND CASTLERIGG FELL

FAIRFIELD AND GREAT LANGDALE FROM PIKE OF BLISCO (above)
THE HOW AND LOUGHRIGG TARN (opposite)

LANGDALE PIKES AND WINDERMERE

LOOKING NORTH FROM SCAFELL PIKE TOWARDS STYHEAD TARN AND DERWENT WATER

GREEN GABLE AND SKIDDAW

16

ELTERWATER, GREAT LANGDALE

17

BROAD CRAG AND GREAT END, WITH GREAT DODD IN THE DISTANCE

BOW FELL AND LITTLE LANGDALE

LITTLE LANGDALE TARN
AND LOUGHRIGG FELL

DAWN MIST NEAR ELTERWATER, GREAT LANGDALE

SKIDDAW AND PIKE OF STICKLE FROM PIKE OF BLISCO (above)
EASDALE TARN FROM BLEA RIGG (opposite)

WINDERMERE AND THE CUMBRIAN MOUNTAINS

WASDALE HEAD, YEWBARROW, MIDDLE FELL AND THE SEA

CALFCLOSE BAY, DERWENT WATER

GRASMERE, BANERIGGS AND HOW TOP

NAB COTTAGE, RYDAL WATER

LATTERBARROW AND WINDERMERE AT DUSK

FAIRFIELD, GREAT RIGG AND HART CRAG FROM LINGMOOR FELL

STRANDSHAG BAY, DERWENT WATER

SKELWITH FOLD AND BLACK FELL, NEAR AMBLESIDE

BLEA TARN AND LANGDALE PIKES

BRIDGE END, LITTLE LANGDALE

WETHERLAM FROM PIKE OF BLISCO

HORSE CRAGS AND LINGMOOR FELL FROM WRYNOSE PASS

HARTER FELL AND HARDKNOTT PASS FROM WRYNOSE PASS

37

HERON PIKE AND FAIRFIELD FROM LOUGHRIGG FELL

HIGH RAISE AND HELM CRAG
FROM ABOVE GRASMERE

CONISTON WATER – LOOKING SOUTH
TOWARDS BLAWITH FELLS

STICKLE TARN AND HARRISON STICKLE

TOWARDS FAIRFIELD FROM LITTLE FELL, LITTLE LANGDALE

SECLUDED HOUSE ON THE SHORE OF WINDERMERE

43

BROTHER'S WATER, NEAR PATTERDALE

PASTURE BOTTOM AND HARTSOP DODD WITH ULLSWATER IN THE DISTANCE

WAST WATER FROM YEWBARROW

DERWENT WATER,
CAT BELLS AND CRAG HILL

MARTINDALE, HOWE GRAIN AND THE NAB WITH HIGH RAISE AND REST DODD IN THE DISTANCE (above)
STANG END, LITTLE LANGDALE (opposite)

49

BOW FELL AND WINDERMERE

GREAT GABLE FROM SCAFELL PIKE

LOUGHRIGG TARN AND LANGDALE PIKES

LANGDALE PIKES FROM ABOVE ELTERWATER, GREAT LANGDALE

STONETHWAITE, EAGLE CRAG AND ULLSCARF

54

CAT BELLS, DERWENT ISLE AND GRISEDALE PIKE ACROSS DERWENT WATER

BOW FELL, ROSSETT PIKE AND PIKE OF STICKLE

LITTLE LANGDALE

57

COLTHOUSE HEIGHTS AND WINDERMERE

HERON ISLAND AND LITTLE ISLE, RYDAL WATER

GREAT GABLE AND WAST WATER

ESKDALE

GRASMERE

LOUGHRIGG TARN

BORROWDALE, GLARAMARA AND GREAT GABLE FROM GRANGE FELL

GRANGE CRAGS AND DERWENT WATER WITH BLENCATHRA IN THE DISTANCE

DOW CRAG AND SEATHWAITE TARN FROM SWIRL HOW

DRYSTONE WALL AND LICHEN

HAYESWATER GILL,
HARTSOP AND HELVELLYN

BOOT BANK, ESKDALE

PIKE OF BLISCO, OXENDALE AND CRINKLE CRAGS

LINGMOOR FELL, PIKE OF BLISCO AND CRINKLE CRAGS FROM NEAR SKELWITH FOLD

LOOKING SOUTH ACROSS DERWENT WATER

SKIDDAW AND DERWENT WATER

ULLSWATER NEAR POOLEY BRIDGE

HELVELLYN

GREENBURN AND TILBERTHWAITE FELLS FROM HELL GILL PIKE (above)
SCA FELL AND SCAFELL PIKE FROM YEWBARROW (opposite)

WETHERLAM AND LITTLE LANGDALE FROM LANG PARROCK

LITTLE LANGDALE

ROSTHWAITE POST OFFICE, BORROWDALE

GREAT LANGDALE AND THE BAND

81

BARROW BAY, DERWENT WATER

SIDE PIKE AND LANGDALE PIKES

83

ULLSWATER, LONG CRAG AND HELVELLYN

THE SHORE OF ULLSWATER NEAR SANDWICK

THE OLD MAN OF CONISTON ACROSS CONISTON WATER

WETHERLAM, WRYNOSE FELL AND
PIKE HOWE FROM NEAR STICKLE TARN

THE SCREES, WAST WATER

WASDALE HEAD

SCAFELL PIKE FROM ABOVE BORROWDALE

WINDERMERE AND TROUTBECK PARK FROM THORNTHWAITE CRAG

BLEA WATER FROM HIGH STREET

MICKLEDEN, ROSSETT PIKE AND LANGDALE PIKES

BOW FELL, LANGDALE PIKES AND WINDERMERE AT DUSK

HAWKSHEAD

STYHEAD TARN, BASE BROWN AND SKIDDAW

96

THIRLMERE AND LONSCALE FELL

BOW FELL AND WINDERMERE FROM SCAFELL PIKE

BOW FELL AND LITTLE LANGDALE TARN

RAMPSHOLME ISLAND, CRAG HILL AND GRISEDALE PIKE ACROSS DERWENT WATER

WATENDLATH TARN

'THE BRITANNIA', ELTERWATER, GREAT LANGDALE

BOW FELL, THE BAND, LANGDALE PIKES AND SIDE PIKE

BUTTERMERE AND CRUMMOCK WATER FROM HAY STACKS

RAYRIGG WYKE, WINDERMERE

ELTER WATER AND LINGMOOR FELL FROM LOUGHRIGG FELL

106

SCA FELL AND SCAFELL PIKE ACROSS WAST WATER

DERWENT WATER AT DUSK

ROSTHWAITE FELL, BORROWDALE

LITTLE LANGDALE TARN AND TILBERTHWAITE FELLS (above)
LANGDALE PIKES (opposite)

CASTLERIGG STONE CIRCLE

Index of Places